D0906545

DEMCO

Franklin D. Roosevelt

Childhoods
of the
Presidents

John Adams

George W. Bush

Bill Clinton

Ulysses S. Grant

Andrew Jackson

Thomas Jefferson

John F. Kennedy

Abraham Lincoln

James Madison

James Monroe

Ronald Reagan

Franklin D. Roosevelt

Theodore Roosevelt

Harry S. Truman

George Washington

Woodrow Wilson

Franklin D. Roosevelt

Anne Marie Sullivan

Mason Crest Publishers
Philadelphia

Produced by OTTN Publishing, Stockton, New Jersey

Mason Crest Publishers
370 Reed Road
Broomall, PA 19008
www.masoncrest.com

First printing

1 3 5 7 9 8 6 4 2

Library of Congress Cataloging-in-Publicat on Data

Sullivan, Anne Marie.
    Franklin D. Roosevelt / Anne Marie Sullivan.
       p.   cm.   (Childhood of the presidents)
    Summary: A biography of the thirty-second president of the
    United States, focusing on his childhood and young adulthood.
    Includes bibliographical references (p.) and index.
       ISBN 1-59084-279-0 (hc.)
    1. Roosevelt, Franklin D. (Franklin Delano), 1882-1945—Juvenile
    literature. 2. Roosevelt, Franklin D. (Franklin Delano), 1882-1945—
    Childhood and youth—Juvenile literature. 3. Presidents—United
    States—Biography—Juvenile literature. [1. Roosevelt, Franklin D.
    (Franklin Delano), 1882-1945—Childhood and youth. 2.
    Presidents.] I. Title. II. Series.
    E807.S897 2003
    973.917'092—dc21
    [B]   2002024447

Publisher's note: All quotations in this book come
from original sources, and contain the spelling and
grammatical inconsistencies of the original text.

Childhoods of the Presidents

Table of Contents

★★★★★★★★★★★★★★★★★★★

★ *Introduction* ★

Alexis de Tocqueville began his great work *Democracy in America* with a discourse on childhood. If we are to understand the prejudices, the habits and the passions that will rule a man's life, Tocqueville said, we must watch the baby in his mother's arms; we must see the first images that the world casts upon the mirror of his mind; we must hear the first words that awaken his sleeping powers of thought. "The entire man," he wrote, "is, so to speak, to be seen in the cradle of the child."

That is why these books on the childhoods of the American presidents are so much to the point. And, as our history shows, a great variety of childhoods can lead to the White House. The record confirms the ancient adage that every American boy, no matter how unpromising his beginnings, can aspire to the presidency. Soon, one hopes, the adage will be extended to include every American girl.

All our presidents thus far have been white males who, within the limits of their gender, reflect the diversity of American life. They were born in nineteen of our states; eight of the last thirteen presidents were born west of the Mississippi. Of all our presidents, Abraham Lincoln had the least promising childhood, yet he became our greatest president. Oddly enough, presidents who are children of privilege sometimes feel an obligation to reform society in order to give children of poverty a better break. And, with Lincoln the great exception, presidents who are children of poverty sometimes feel that there is no need to reform a society that has enabled them to rise from privation to the summit.

Does schooling make a difference? Harry S. Truman, the only twentieth-century president never to attend college, is generally accounted a near-great president. Actually nine— more than one fifth—of our presidents never went to college at all, including such luminaries as George Washington, Andrew Jackson and Grover Cleveland. But, Truman aside, all the non-college men held the highest office before the twentieth century, and, given the increasing complexity of life, a college education will unquestionably be a necessity in the twenty-first century.

Every reader of this book, girls included, has a right to aspire to the presidency. As you survey the childhoods of those who made it, try to figure out the qualities that brought them to the White House. I would suggest that among those qualities are ambition, determination, discipline, education— and luck.

—*ARTHUR M. SCHLESINGER, JR.*

1

One of the earliest photographs of Franklin Delano Roosevelt, who was born into wealth and privilege in Hyde Park, New York, in 1882.

A Small Child in a Small World

igh on a snow-covered hill overlooking the Hudson River stood a large, comfortable wooden house with a porch and a three-story tower. Acres of trees, a thriving farm, and stables of fine horses surrounded the house. This was Springwood, the home of James and Sara Delano Roosevelt.

On the night of January 30, 1882, a newborn baby's cry could be heard coming from one of the upstairs bedrooms. After a long and difficult labor, Sara had given birth to her first and only child, a boy weighing 10 pounds. Sara was James's second wife. She was in her mid-twenties and James in his early fifties when they married several years after the death of James's first wife. He had a son by his first marriage, James Roosevelt, known as Rosy.

It would be some time before James and Sara would agree upon a name for their new baby. They finally settled on Franklin Delano Roosevelt, after Sara's uncle. This was the name given to the baby at his *christening* on March 20, 1882, at St. James *Episcopal* Church in Hyde Park, New York, not far from Springwood. One of Franklin's godparents was his father's distant cousin Elliott Roosevelt, whose brother

Franklin Roosevelt's most distinguished relative was Theodore Roosevelt, who is considered one of the greatest U.S. presidents. Like Franklin, Theodore Roosevelt had been born into a wealthy New York family, and grew up in an atmosphere of wealth and privilege.

Theodore would one day become the 26th president of the United States.

Little Franklin was born into a small and privileged world. The Roosevelts were among the oldest and most respected families in New York. They had descended from one of the original Dutch settlers of the area and were known as *Knickerbockers*. In addition to their very old family ties to the area, the Roosevelts enjoyed great wealth. So did many of their neighbors. In fact, the area of the Hudson River where Springwood was located became known as "Millionaire's Row." Many of the richest and most powerful families in New York City chose to build their lavish country estates there. Sara's family, the Delanos, had a lot of money as well. They had made a fortune in the shipping business in New England. Sara's father, Warren Delano, also had an estate on the Hudson, known as Algonac.

Much of the wealth in the United States at that time was concentrated in the hands of a few powerful families. Of these, the wealthiest and most powerful was the Astor family. Every year, Mrs. Caroline Astor held a ball to which only 400 people were invited. These 400, in a city of 1.2 million people, were considered the upper crust of New York society. Franklin's parents were always invited. In fact, Franklin's half brother, Rosy, was married to one of Mrs. Astor's daughters.

New York's powerful families formed a small social circle that followed the same comfortable routines year after year. They spent the coldest months of the winter in their city

A society gathering, late 1800s or early 1900s. Because the Roosevelts traveled in the most exclusive social circles, Franklin's childhood included almost no contact with anyone outside the upper-class elite.

Franklin with his mother, Sara Delano Roosevelt, who doted on her only child. Other parents in the Roosevelts' social circle often left the care of their children up to servants, but Sara was very involved in taking care of her son.

homes attending dances, parties, and the theater with other members of the same group. Many could be found at their country estates during the more pleasant months. Here, they pursued outdoor pleasures such as riding horses and hunting. It was also quite common for these families to own summer homes on the coast and travel frequently to Europe. Even overseas, the families remained within their own social group, finding one another on the same luxurious ships and at the same European resorts.

Franklin's parents followed this pattern closely. In addition to Springwood, they owned a home on Campobello Island, just off the coasts of Maine and New Brunswick, Canada. When they were in the United States, they spent their summers there. They also lived in New York City for part of the year. They left the United States often, however, for both Sara and James loved to travel. The first year of their marriage, they spent 10 months in Europe. Their habits did not change when Franklin joined the family. He crossed the Atlantic with his parents many times as a very small child.

In some ways, Sara was different from other mothers in her social class. All her friends and relatives hired nurses, nannies, and *governesses* to care for their children. Most of these parents pursued very busy social lives and left the care and daily routines of their children to the servants. They often left the children at home when they traveled. Many women observed a "mother's hour," the one regular time during the day that they spent with their children.

James and Sara had servants to care for Franklin, as well. But Sara liked to take care of him herself. She and James took Franklin nearly everywhere they went, rarely leaving him home with the servants. "I used to love to bathe and dress [Franklin]," Sara wrote. "I felt . . . that every mother ought to learn to care for her own baby, whether she can afford to delegate the task to some one else or not." From the beginning, James and

When Franklin married at age 23, his distant cousin Theodore Roosevelt—then the president of the United States—gave the bride away. The bride was Anna Eleanor Roosevelt (who was most often called simply Eleanor), the president's niece and daughter of Franklin's god-father, Elliott Roosevelt.

Sara delighted in Franklin. He was "a very nice child," James wrote, ". . . always bright and happy. Not crying, worrying."

The Roosevelts' vacation home on Campobello Island. Here Franklin spent many of his summers, both during his childhood and in later life.

Little Franklin entered a safe, sheltered world in which his parents adored him. Aside from servants, he hardly ever met anyone who didn't belong to his parents' close circle of friends and relations. Of course, his was hardly the typical childhood for an American boy at the time.

The Roosevelts were one of the oldest families in New York at a time when America's cities were greeting waves of new-comers. Immigrants from other countries were pouring into New York City by the millions. While Franklin was growing up in the country, surrounded by acres of farm and wooded land in Hyde Park, many people were leaving the country to seek factory jobs in the cities.

As the cities grew, they became crowded. Many people lived in *tenements*—very crowded, often dirty apartment houses. While Franklin's family enjoyed a leisurely life traveling from one pleasant location to another, many people were working very long hours for low wages in factories. Instead of going to school and playing outdoors, many children began working at an early age to help support their families. Workers were beginning to form *unions*, organizations that would help them gain better pay and working conditions.

Franklin's parents, however, were not interested in change. They were content to continue living the life they knew, and they expected Franklin's life to be much like theirs. Years later, Sara was asked whether she had ever expected her son to become president one day. She responded, "Never, oh never! . . . What was my ambition for him? . . . It was

> As president, Franklin Roosevelt would help the poor and unemployed through his New Deal job creation and social support programs. The resulting higher taxes on the rich led them to brand him "a traitor to his class."

the highest ideal I could hold up before our boy—to grow to be like his father, straight and honorable, just and kind, an upstanding American."

As a child, Franklin accompanied his father on the elder Roosevelt's daily horseback inspections of Springwood, the family's Hyde Park estate. Sara Roosevelt rounds out this photo with a family dog.

Early Confidence

Many years later, Sara Roosevelt recalled an incident from her son's childhood that summed up the quiet self-assurance Franklin Delano Roosevelt displayed throughout his life. Franklin had been playing among the trees by the river in Hyde Park when he spied a winter wren. He wanted to add the tiny bird to his collection.

He returned to the house to grab his gun. Curious, his mother, whom he called "Mummie," asked why he wanted the gun. When she heard his answer, she smiled, trying to hold in her laughter. "And do you think that wren is going to oblige you by staying there while you come in and get your gun to go back and shoot him?" she asked.

"Oh yes," Franklin replied. "He'll wait."

Mummie shook her head, still smiling, as Franklin took his time strolling back down the lawn toward the river. She looked forward to some gentle teasing when he returned empty-handed, for the bird would surely not wait. In a short while, Franklin did return, but Mummie could not tease him. He held the tiny dead bird in his hand. Franklin was entirely confident that everything would go his way, and this bird, as

Franklin Roosevelt was the only president in U.S. history to be elected to four terms. After his death, an amendment to the Constitution was passed limiting presidents to two terms.

expected, did exactly as he wished.

Franklin's parents helped him to develop this confidence. From the time he was born, they surrounded him with their love, attention, and approval. They enjoyed everything he did, writing it all faithfully in Sara's daily diary. Even in a situation that could have been terrifying, Sara and James managed to keep Franklin warm, safe, and calm. When Franklin was three, the ship on which he and his parents were traveling home from England was hit by a huge wave. As water began to seep under their cabin door, Sara and James did not panic. Instead, Sara wrapped Franklin in her fur coat, explaining to James that if her "poor little boy . . . must go down," she was determined he would be "going down warm." Fortunately, the ship did not sink, making it back to England damaged but in one piece.

When he was small, Franklin enjoyed following his mother around as she managed the household. He felt shy with the cook and some of the other servants, hiding behind his mother's skirts when they tried to talk to him or tempt him with treats. James also brought Franklin along when he made his daily rounds on horseback of the property at Springwood. James loved horses and built fine stables at Springwood for the horses he raised and kept on the property. At first, James held Franklin on his own saddle during the morning ride. But as soon as the boy was old enough to sit on a horse's back,

James gave him a small Welsh pony. By the time Franklin was four, he was riding alongside his father every morning.

James also taught Franklin how to sled in the winter and sail in the summer. The Roosevelts' sailboat was named the *Half Moon*. This was also the name of the ship in which Henry Hudson had explored the Hudson River during the early 17th century, in the days before the Dutch settled New York. Franklin loved to sail, and many of his games involved dreams of adventure on the high seas. He became an expert sailor. When he was older, his parents presented him with his own small sailboat. He named her the *New Moon* in honor of his father's boat.

Franklin (center) aboard the *New Moon*, the small sailboat his parents gave him. He loved taking the boat out on the Hudson River.

This view of the mansion at Hyde Park gives an idea of the splendor of Franklin Roosevelt's childhood home.

Another outdoor activity that James enjoyed was hunting. Sara was worried when James gave Franklin his own gun when he was only 11. Franklin was delighted. He was fascinated with natural history and loved to collect things. He decided to shoot one bird of every species that lived in the Hudson River valley. He even learned to preserve and stuff them himself. Sara proudly displayed his bird collection at Springwood, dusting it herself rather than allowing the servants to do so.

Sara would insist that because young Franklin never gave her or James any trouble, they hardly ever needed to discipline him. He spent his early years performing for a very appreciative adult audience and disliked causing unpleasantness or fuss for his parents. He tried even harder to keep from worrying them after James suffered a heart attack when Franklin was eight. James's health never fully returned. Franklin often traveled with his parents to a German *spa* called Bad Nauheim, where James hoped to find a cure. Franklin developed a habit of showing his parents the positive side of everything and trying to hide or make light of any problems he might be facing. He once broke a tooth, uncovering the nerve. Although it must have been horribly painful, he tried to hide his condition from his mother, mumbling and trying not to open his mouth until she demanded to see it.

Until he turned 14, Franklin's world revolved around his parents and his home on the Hudson River. Wealthy children rarely attended elementary school in those days. Instead, they received private lessons from governesses and tutors. As an only child who lived in the country, Franklin spent most of his time with adults or playing on his own.

There were children in the neighborhood—many of the people who worked on the estate had children, and many children lived in the town of Hyde Park. But these youngsters lived outside Franklin's social world, and

Franklin's love of collecting and inability to throw anything away led him to establish the nation's first presidential library at Hyde Park in 1938. Inside Springwood, Franklin's bedroom and bird collection remain unchanged.

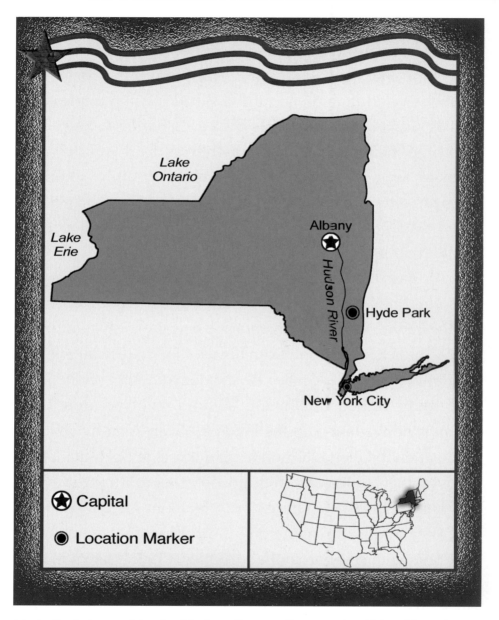

Hyde Park, located in the Hudson River valley north of New York City, lies in the heart of what was called "Millionaire's Row."

he had no chance to play with them. Instead, his playmates were the few other wealthy children who lived on estates in the neighborhood. He also played with Helen and Taddy

Roosevelt, Rosy's children, when they were visiting or when the families met in Europe. Although they were actually his half niece and nephew, Helen and Taddy were close to Franklin's age.

Franklin had no brothers or sisters but plenty of cousins on both sides of the family. Both the Roosevelts and the Delanos maintained close family ties. They gathered together for holidays and house parties, staying in one another's homes. On these occasions, Franklin had more chance to be around other children than he ever had at home. Sara remembered one of these parties at Springwood when Franklin was four. His godfather, Elliott Roosevelt, was visiting with his family. Elliott's two-year-old daughter, Eleanor, was feeling shy until Franklin asked her if she'd like to play horse. They spent the rest of the afternoon in the nursery with Eleanor riding around on Franklin's back.

When he did have the opportunity to play with other children, Franklin's mother noticed that he tended to take charge of the games. He was not used to sharing his toys, taking turns, or making any of the other compromises children learn to make when they play together. His games were his own. Other children usually listened to Franklin when he gave orders, according to his mother. One day, she pulled him aside and warned him that he should give the other children a chance. "Mummie," he protested, "if I didn't give the orders, nothing would happen!" From an early age, Franklin was confident that the world would respond to his will. Much as he was sure the little wren would not spoil his plans, he was certain his playmates would follow along with his designs.

A portrait of father and son. James Roosevelt, in his early fifties when he married Sara Delano, would suffer his first heart attack when Franklin was eight years old.

A Class of One

*B*efore he was seven, Franklin learned the alphabet from his mother and picked up the basics of reading and writing at home. He enjoyed writing little notes to his mother, which she saved. After that, he began traveling to Crumwold, the estate next to Springwood, for two hours every day. There he had lessons with the neighbors' children, Archie and Edmund Rogers, given by their German governess. During the years when most children today go to elementary school, Franklin was taught privately by a number of governesses, all of them from Europe. From them, he learned German and French, along with his other subjects. These teachers traveled with the family, so Sara and James did not have to plan their trips around school vacations or leave Franklin behind. He could have his lessons anywhere in the world.

While Franklin was still a baby, his parents had placed his name on the waiting list for Groton School, a private college preparatory school for boys in Massachusetts. The school had been founded around that time by the Reverend Endicott Peabody, an Episcopal minister. Peabody dreamed of creating a private school where he could educate the sons of the wealthy according to Christian principles. He placed great importance on physical development and encouraged athletics. Most of all, he, along with his wife, hoped to cultivate a family atmosphere at Groton. James probably liked the idea of sending his son to a school where religion was emphasized. He was a devout Episcopalian and a faithful member of St. James Church in Hyde Park. In addition to serving for many years on the *vestry*, a committee of congregation members, James took up the collection at services every Sunday.

Most boys started Groton when they were 12 and studied there for six years until they were ready for college. But Groton was a boarding school. Students lived there and went home only for school holidays. Despite their enthusiasm for the school, Franklin's parents were not ready to be separated from him when he was 12. Instead, they hired a male tutor to prepare him for Groton and kept him home for another two years.

But Sara and James finally agreed that Franklin needed to be around boys his own age. "The time had come when we could no longer allow our desire to keep him with us to limit his scope of experiences," Sara later admitted. So when the family returned home from a trip to Europe, Franklin's parents prepared to send him off to Groton School. They had planned it this way since Franklin was a tiny boy, but now Sara faced it "with a heavy heart."

Even Sara admitted that Franklin was starting school at a disadvantage. He would begin Groton in the third year (known there as the third form) instead of the first because his parents had waited the extra two years. Most of the other boys in his class had started together two years earlier. They had made their friends when they were all new together. Now, Franklin would stand alone as the new boy. Sara worried, knowing that Franklin had been shy with strangers ever since the days when he clung to her skirts in the kitchen at Springwood.

> As an adult Franklin, like his father, suffered from health problems that he tried to cure at a spa. After his bout with polio, a disease that left him partially paralyzed, he loved bathing in the hot waters of Warm Springs, Georgia.

Sara's worries were not unfounded. Franklin was beginning a completely different life from anything he had known before. At 14 years old, he would enter a world where he was no longer sheltered by his parents' constant love and approval. He would have to stand on his own and compete with other boys on an equal footing for the first time in his life. He was always so confident everything would go his way, and he had rarely been disappointed. How would his confidence stand up to the rough, competitive environment of an all-boys school?

If defeats and disappointments at Groton ever crushed Franklin's spirit, Sara would never discover this from his letters. He was always so attuned to his parents' feelings that he was sure to write what he knew they wanted to hear. His letters home reported the news fairly accurately, good and bad. But he never revealed any deep feelings in these letters. He laughed off his problems or made excuses. Sara was forced to sit and wonder what Franklin was doing from a distance. Her picture of what was happening was his version of events. For the first time, Franklin's life would not revolve completely around his parents.

The World of Groton

*I*n the middle of September 1896, Franklin and his parents arrived at Groton in their private railroad car. After settling Franklin in his room, Sara and James returned home alone. "It is hard to leave my darling boy," Sara wrote in her diary when she reached home. Franklin, however, never wrote about how being left at Groton made him feel. In fact, he rarely revealed how he felt about anything at Groton. If, like many teenagers, he wanted to be the most popular boy, the best athlete, and the top student, he was probably disappointed. Still, he would always remember his years at Groton warmly. He admired the *headmaster*, the Reverend Endicott Peabody, enormously. They continued to exchange letters through the years, and Franklin sometimes quoted Peabody in his speeches. Franklin also would ask Peabody to perform his wedding ceremony.

Every morning after breakfast, Groton students attended chapel, where Peabody gave a religious lesson. In addition

Franklin Roosevelt (standing, center) as team manager for the Groton School's baseball club. When Franklin turned 14, his parents reluctantly decided to send him to the exclusive boarding school in Massachusetts—his first school—because they believed he needed to be around other boys.

to his duties as headmaster of the school, Peabody served as *rector*, or head minister, at Groton. He was as much his students' spiritual leader as their leader in academics, and maybe more so. Peabody taught all the classes in religion, which was a required subject at Groton. In chapel and at his lessons, Franklin absorbed Peabody's beliefs, which mirrored the faith that his parents had introduced to him.

Franklin's wife, Eleanor, later wrote of his religious beliefs, "He had a strong religious feeling and his religion was a very personal one. I think he actually felt he could ask God for guidance and receive it." No one ever knew him to suffer any religious doubt. Franklin's confident religious faith may have been the source of his constant optimism and fearlessness.

The furnishings at Groton were plain and practical, not luxurious. The wealthy boys had to adjust to more basic surroundings than they were used to at home. The days were constantly busy and highly structured. The boys took two cold showers every day—one in the morning, one in the evening. Classes were followed by sports, then study time after supper. After evening prayers, the headmaster and his wife shook every boy's hand, wishing each one good night.

In addition to religion, Franklin studied Latin, Greek, French, English, history, algebra, and science at Groton. He had no trouble with his schoolwork. His governesses and tutors had done their job well, and he arrived at school at the same level as his classmates. In a class of 19, Franklin ranked fourth his first term.

Unfortunately, Franklin found it harder to succeed at fitting in than at his schoolwork. He had not spent much time with boys his own age, and he had never really had to compete for anything before. Starting school later than everyone else in his class just made breaking into the group that much harder. Up to this point, his life had focused on pleasing adults. Now he had to learn how to appeal to people his own age. It took him a while to realize that being good all the time isn't the best way to earn the respect of other boys. Toward the end of his first year, Franklin finally received his first "black mark" for bad behavior—talking in class. He wrote the news to his parents, sounding relieved. He admitted, "I was thought to have no school spirit before."

Being a good athlete was a surefire road to success and popularity at Groton. At a school where athletics ruled, football was the king of all sports. Unfortunately for Franklin, he matured later than some of the other boys. When he arrived at Groton, he was smaller than most of his classmates, and he was always thin. A childhood spent playing by himself or with a few other children hadn't prepared him well for team sports. He made the second-worst football team and the worst baseball team. He also tried boxing, without much success.

Franklin tried to make up for his lack of athletic skill with intense school spirit. He may not have made the top football team, but no one cheered louder when they beat their rival, St. Mark's. Franklin was taller by his fourth-form year—he was six feet one inch tall by the time he graduated—but he remained thin. He would never be good at team sports. In his final year, he decided that he could manage the baseball team even if he wasn't much of a player. It was a difficult and boring job, but Franklin handled it well.

Franklin found more success on the debating team than on the athletic field. All those years of conversation with adults had prepared him to shine in any competition that involved talking. He also joined the Groton choir and, to his great joy, landed a role in the school play in his sixth-form year. He played an old, deaf character named Uncle Bopaddy in a play called *The Wedding March*. He enjoyed performing and was very funny in the role, according to the reviews.

Through his interest in the Groton Missionary Society, Franklin came into close contact with people outside his social class, for the first time in his life. This club's purpose was to extend charity to people in need. The club ran a summer camp for poor boys from Boston. Franklin spent two weeks as a counselor at the camp the summer before he started college. Along with his closest friend at Groton, Lathrop Brown, Franklin was also given the duty of looking after an elderly black woman who lived near the school. They checked on her regularly, did chores, and shoveled snow for her.

James and Sara believed in the duty of privileged people to help those who have less. They tried to instill this belief in Franklin as well. Groton's headmaster added another dimension to the idea. Endicott Peabody stressed the duty of public service to his students. He hoped that many of them would enter politics and bring the ideals that he had taught them into the service of government.

Franklin's ears were wide open to this message. He practically worshiped his cousin Theodore Roosevelt, whom Rector Peabody often invited to speak at Groton's chapel. During Franklin's years at Groton, Theodore Roosevelt became assis-

Decked out in a top hat and phony beard, Franklin Roosevelt can be seen at right in this photo from Groton's 1900 production of the play *The Wedding March*. According to reviews from the time, the future president was quite funny in his role as Uncle Bopaddy.

tant secretary of the navy. When the Spanish-American War broke out in 1898, he left this job to fight in Cuba with a *cavalry* unit called the Rough Riders. They soon became famous for their bravery in battle and were treated as heroes by the American people. While Franklin was still at Groton, Theodore Roosevelt was elected governor of New York. He became vice president of the United States not long after Franklin's graduation. His accomplishments helped attract Franklin to public life.

Theodore Roosevelt became a national hero by leading the Rough Riders' charge up San Juan Hill. Scarlet fever cut short Franklin's improbable dream of sharing in his distant cousin's wartime glory.

His cousin's example also inspired Franklin and Lathrop Brown to hatch a wild scheme when the fighting started in Cuba. They planned to run away from school and join the navy. Franklin had loved boats and sailing all his life. He once mentioned to his father that he would like to go to the U.S. Naval Academy at Annapolis. James Roosevelt was against the idea, preferring that his son attend Harvard. Franklin's dreams of glory at sea got no further this time. Before they had the chance to carry out their plan, Franklin and Lathrop came down with scarlet fever and landed in the Groton *infirmary*.

Sara and James had just arrived at Bad Nauheim when they heard that Franklin's illness looked serious. They caught the first ship home. When they arrived at Groton, Sara was told that Franklin was contagious and no visitors were allowed. To get around this problem, she climbed a ladder several times a day. Sitting at the top of the ladder next to Franklin's window, she could see and talk to him. When he was well enough, Sara took Franklin to Springwood to recuperate. He was completely well by the time he went back to Groton the next fall.

Franklin experienced disappointment for the first time in his life during his years at Groton. Although he was good, he was not the best. For example, in his sixth-form year Franklin was picked as a dormitory *prefect*, an older boy the teachers trusted to look after the younger ones. Although he was pleased with the honor, it wasn't enough. He had high hopes that Rector Peabody would also choose him to be a senior prefect, one of the boys considered most qualified to be school leaders. To Franklin's bitter disappointment, he never made senior prefect. He did, however, win the Latin Prize at his graduation from Groton.

When Franklin left Groton, he was already enrolled at Harvard and planning to room with Lathrop Brown. At the beginning of December during his freshman year, Franklin received an urgent message from Sara asking him to come to New York City right away. His father's health had been getting steadily worse. The whole family was together when James died on December 8, 1900. When Franklin returned to Harvard in January, Sara was on her own.

A Roosevelt campaign poster. Elected to the presidency four times, FDR would lead the United States through depression and war.

Leading a Frightened Nation

While still at Harvard, Franklin became engaged to Eleanor Roosevelt. The two were married on March 17, 1905. Eleanor was deeply interested in social problems and improving life for all people in America. Although she grew up in the same *insulated* society as Franklin, her interests helped introduce him to problems in the wider world.

After Franklin graduated from Harvard, he enrolled in law school at Columbia University in New York City. He practiced law for a few years, but in 1910 the local Democratic Party persuaded Franklin to run for the New York State Senate. To everyone's surprise but his own, he won. In 1913 the newly elected Democratic president, Woodrow Wilson, appointed Franklin assistant secretary of the navy. Always fascinated by the navy, Franklin enjoyed this job and became known as a good administrator.

In 1920 the national Democratic Party asked Franklin to run for vice president of the United States. Unfortunately for him, the Republican candidates, Warren G. Harding and Calvin Coolidge, won easily. However, this election gave Franklin good experience at running a national campaign.

Franklin returned to practicing law until he fell ill during his summer vacation at Campobello Island in 1921. After a few days, it became clear that he'd been stricken by *polio*, a serious viral illness. Until a vaccine was developed in the 1950s, polio left many of its victims paralyzed. When Franklin began to recover, he found that he could no longer move from the waist down.

In 1928, Franklin was pressured to run for governor of New York. He was reluctant at first but finally agreed. After spending seven years searching for a cure for his paralysis, he still could not move his legs. He felt he had to prove to the voters that his handicap would have no effect on his fitness for the job. Franklin developed ways to deal gracefully with his handicap that he would use throughout his career in politics. He used metal leg braces to stand, firmly holding onto a podium, a metal bar, or a strong arm. He tried to give speeches standing up whenever possible, and even managed to walk short distances by wearing his braces and tightly gripping another man's arm. At a time when buildings had no handicapped access, Franklin often had to be carried up steps. Still, he always tried to appear as strong as possible in public. Although he used a wheelchair in private, he didn't want to be filmed or photographed in it, and the press respected his wishes.

Franklin won the election. During his first term as governor, the stock market crashed, triggering the *Great Depression*. Individuals and companies saw a great deal of their money wiped out in one day. By the end of Franklin's second term as governor, one-fourth of the country's workers had no jobs. People were desperate.

Eleanor Roosevelt on the day of her wedding to her distant cousin Franklin Delano Roosevelt. A remarkable person in her own right, Eleanor was a lifelong champion for the underprivileged.

Franklin was elected president of the United States in 1932 in the midst of this dark time. He immediately tried to calm the frightened nation. "The only thing we have to fear," he said in his first speech as president, "is fear itself." Americans took comfort in the confidence their president displayed. It was a confidence that Franklin Roosevelt had shown ever since his childhood years.

Believing that government had the power not simply to calm its citizens in a crisis but also to solve problems, Franklin quickly started fighting the economic chaos. During his first 100 days in office, he convinced Congress to pass many laws designed to stabilize the economy. Franklin told the American people he was offering them a "New Deal."

New Deal programs tried to create jobs, as well as a safety net for people who were unable to work. Many of these

The last color photo taken of President Roosevelt, January 6, 1945, shows the toll more than three years of war had taken on him physically. Three months later a brain hemorrhage would claim his life.

programs, such as Social Security, still exist today. Some New Deal programs helped, but Franklin's personality was just as important in pulling the nation together. Eleanor Roosevelt wrote, "I never knew [Franklin] to face Lfe, or any problem that came up, with fear, and I have often wondered if that courageous attitude was not communicated to the people of the country. It may well be what helped them to pull themselves out of the depression in the first years of his administration. . . . He believed in the courage and ability of men, and they responded."

While Americans focused on their own problems during the depression, the rest of the world was facing another emergency. Adolf Hitler and his Nazi Party had come to power in Germany in 1933. After expanding Germany's borders through agreements and the threat of violence, Hitler ordered his armies to invade Poland in 1939. This touched off World War II, the bloodiest war in history. As Germany conquered country after country in Europe, Germany's *ally*, Japan, was trying to take over China. Many Americans sympathized with the Chinese and with the countries fighting Germany, but most Americans did not want to enter the war.

Everything changed after the Japanese attacked the American naval base at Pearl Harbor in Hawaii on December 7, 1941. Franklin called it "a day which will live in infamy." Now no one argued that the United States should not get involved in World War II. It was up to Franklin to lead the nation through another crisis. Almost overnight, the whole country began working to build up the military and make supplies for the war.

By 1945, it was clear Germany and Japan were going to be defeated. Much of the world had been torn apart by the long war, and many European nations had no real governments after being occupied by the Germans for so long. It was time to plan for peace. Franklin had already agreed, along with the leaders of several other nations, to form an international orga-nization that would help countries work out their differences peacefully. The United Nations charter was signed in June of 1945, and a majority of countries agreed to it by October.

Unfortunately, Franklin did not live to see the birth of the United Nations or the end of the war. In April, Franklin retreated to the spa at Warm Springs, Georgia, to rest. On April 12, 1945, he collapsed from a brain *hemorrhage* and died. Though she was not in Warm Springs when her husband died, Eleanor knew his courage and his deep religious faith well. "I am sure that he died looking into the future as calmly as he had looked at all the events of his life," she wrote.

CHRONOLOGY

1882   Franklin Delano Roosevelt is born on January 30 at Springwood in Hyde Park, New York.

1890   Father, James Roosevelt, suffers his first heart attack.

1896   Franklin enrolls at Groton School.

1900   James Roosevelt dies.

1903   Franklin is awarded bachelor of arts degree from Harvard University.

1905   Marries distant cousin Anna Eleanor Roosevelt.

1910   Elected to the New York State Senate.

1913   Appointed assistant secretary of the United States Navy.

1920   Runs for vice president of the United States on the Democratic ticket.

1921   Contracts polio and becomes paralyzed from the waist down.

1928   Elected governor of New York.

1929   The stock market crashes, plunging America—and the rest of the world—into the Great Depression.

1932   Franklin D. Roosevelt is elected president of the United States.

1941   The Japanese attack Pearl Harbor; the United States enters World War II.

1945   Franklin Roosevelt dies at Warm Springs, Georgia, on April 12, during his fourth term as president; on May 8, Germany surrenders, ending fighting in Europe; on August 15, Japan surrenders, ending World War II; the United Nations is born on October 24.

ally—a country that supports another country, often officially through an agreement or treaty.

cavalry—troops mounted on horseback or moving in motor vehicles.

christening—a Christian ceremony in which an infant is baptized and named.

Episcopal—a type of Protestant Christian church in the United States, similar to the Church of England.

governess—a woman employed to educate and train the children of a private household.

Great Depression—a period of enormous economic stagnation and widespread unemployment, which began in 1929 and lasted throughout the 1930s.

headmaster—the head of a private school, similar to a principal in a public school.

hemorrhage—a large, rapid discharge of blood from the blood vessels.

infirmary—a specific area where the sick stay for care and treatment.

insulated—isolated or protected from the problems and concerns of others.

Knickerbocker—a descendant of the early Dutch settlers of New York.

polio—an infectious viral disease that can attack the nerves of the spinal cord, causing paralysis, atrophy of the muscles, and sometimes deformity.

prefect—a student officer, especially in a private school.

rector—a clergyman in charge of an individual church and its members.

spa—a resort that has pools of mineral-filled spring water thought to promote healing.

tenement—a building divided into apartments for rent to families, especially one meeting only minimum standards of comfort and safety.

union—an organization of workers formed to advance its members' interests, especially in respect to wages and working conditions.

vestry—a committee composed of members of a parish or congregation that oversees the activities of the parish or congregation.

FURTHER READING

Asbell, Bernard. *The F.D.R. Memoirs.* New York: Doubleday & Company, Inc., 1973.

Davis, Kenneth S. *FDR, The War President: A History.* New York: Random House, 2000.

Reynolds, David. *From Munich to Pearl Harbor: Roosevelt's America and the Origins of the Second World War.* New York: Ivan R. Dee, Inc., 2001.

Roosevelt, Eleanor. *This I Remember.* New York: Harper & Brothers, 1949.

Roosevelt, Mrs. James. *My Boy Franklin.* New York: Ray Long & Richard R. Smith, Inc., 1933.

Schlesinger, Arthur M., jr., editor. *The Election of 1932.* Philadelphia: Mason Crest Publishers, 2003.

Ward, Geoffrey C. *Before the Trumpet.* New York: Harper & Row Publishers, 1985.

- http://lcweb2.loc.gov/ammem/ndlpedu/features/timeline/index.html
  American Memory Timeline Home Page

- http://www.feri.org
  Franklin Delano Roosevelt: President of the Century

- http://www.fdrlibrary.marist.edu
  Franklin D. Roosevelt Library and Digital Archives

- http://www.hvnet.com/houses/fdr/
  Hudson Valley Network Historic Houses

- http://www.newdeal.feri.org
  The New Deal Network

INDEX

INDEX

PICTURE CREDITS

Contributors

ARTHUR M. SCHLESINGER JR. holds the Albert Schweitzer Chair in the Humanities at the Graduate Center of the City University of New York. He is the author of more than a dozen books, including *The Age of Jackson*; *The Vital Center*; *The Age of Roosevelt* (3 vols.); *A Thousand Days: John F. Kennedy in the White House*; *Robert Kennedy and His Times*; *The Cycles of American History*; and *The Imperial Presidency*. Professor Schlesinger served as

Special Assistant to President Kennedy (1961–63). His numerous awards include the Pulitzer Prize for History; the Pulitzer Prize for Biography; two National Book Awards; the Bancroft Prize; and the American Academy of Arts and Letters Gold Medal for History.

ANNE MARIE SULLIVAN received her bachelor cf arts degree from Temple University. She has worked in the publishing industry as a writer and editor. She lives with her husband. Ed, and their three children in the Philadelphia suburbs.